LANDSLIDES AND AVALANCHES

Terry Jennings

Belitha Press

First published in Great Britain in 1999 by

Belitha Press Limited,
London House, Great Eastern Wharf,
Parkgate Road, London SW11 4NQ

Produced for Belitha Press Limited by Bender Richardson White
Editors: Lionel Bender and Clare Oliver
Designer: Ben White
Electronic make-up: Mike Weintroub
Illustrator: Rudi Vizi
Picture researchers: Cathy Stastny and Daniela Marceddu
Consultant: Stephen Watts

ISBN 1 84138 057 1

Printed in Singapore

British Library Cataloguing in Publication Data
CIP data for this book is available from the British Library.

Photographic credits
Tony Stone Images: 7 Barbara Filet, 11b David Woodfall, 16l Jacques Jangoux,
26t Robert Van Der Hilst, 26b Rhonda Klevansky. **Rex Features:** 13t, 22 Champlong-
Arepi, 23t Sipa Press/Paris-Tschaen, 25 and front cover Toby Rankin. **Corbis Images:** 4
Marc Garanger, 16r Galen Rowell, 17 Danny Lehman, 21 Galen Rowell. **Terry
Jennings:** 1, 8, 11t, 14, back cover. **Gamma/Frank Spooner Pictures:** cover Bosio-
Figaro magazine, 5t Noel Quidu, 5b Alexandre Sassaki, 13b Chip Hires, 23b Bosio-
Figaro magazine, 29t G. Hinterleitner. **Environmental Images:** 9 Colin Cumming, 29b
Martin Bond. **Oxford Scientific Films:** 28 Colin Monteath. **Science Photo Library:**
15 US Bureau of Reclamation. **John Cleare Mountain Camera:** 18, 19. **Ecoscene:**
24 Nick Hawkes. **PA News:** 20 EPA photos.

Words in **bold** appear in the glossary on pages 30 and 31.

Contents

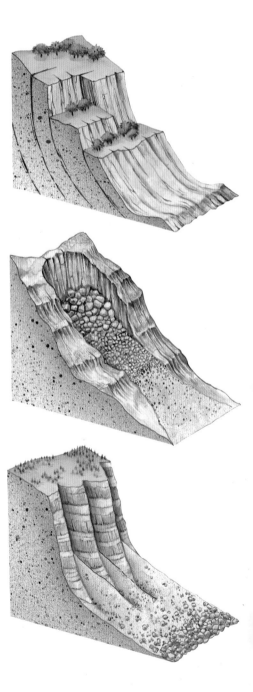

Moving earth

For millions of years, huge slabs of rock in the **Earth's crust** have been forced upwards, to form hills and mountains. Oceans and seas wear away the edges of land to form high cliffs. But wherever there are hills, mountains and cliffs the weather wears them away, and this may cause **landslides**.

Snow and ice

Snow and ice build up on the tops of high mountains. As the snow and ice form thicker and thicker layers, they may start to slide down the side of the mountain. Thousands of tonnes of snow and ice can form an **avalanche** that crashes down the mountain into the **valley** below.

◄ *An avalanche occurs when a huge amount of snow begins to slip down the side of a mountain and crashes into the valley below. This avalanche happened in the French Alps.*

Volcanoes and mudslides

Many **volcanoes** are so high that they have snow on their tops. When one of these volcanoes erupts, the heat melts the snow around its top. The melted snow then mixes with ash from the volcano, forming a huge pile of mud that slides down the side of the volcano. Heavy rain on the slopes of bare hills and mountains often causes **mudslides**, too.

▲ *This mudslide was caused by several days of heavy rain in the highlands of Honduras. People, animals and vehicles were buried in mud.*

▲ *A landslide has destroyed these flimsy houses built on a hillside in Rio de Janeiro, Brazil.*

Destruction

Landslides, avalanches and mudslides can destroy buildings and injure or kill people. They also change the shape of the land.

In this book we show how these natural disasters are caused, and how they affect people and the landscape. We also see what we can do to stop these disasters from happening or to reduce their impact.

How landslides occur

Landslides are huge masses of rock, soil or mud falling very quickly down a slope. They can be started by heavy rain, frost, melting snow or by an **earthquake**. Sometimes a layer of air is trapped under the falling rock or soil, which then floats along like a high-speed hovercraft. Landslides of rock occur where pieces of rock have been broken away from the side of the mountain, hill or cliff.

Weathering

Rocks may appear tough, but many of them are soft and **porous**, while others have cracks in them.

In cool, wet climates, water that collects in these pores and cracks may later freeze. As the water freezes, it expands and takes up more room. The ice presses against the sides of each pore or crack.

On high mountains, water often freezes at night and the ice melts the next day. This process can happen over and over again. The ice slowly widens the cracks in the rock until pieces begin to break off. In addition, rainwater is slightly **acidic**. This acid slowly softens some rocks, such as chalk, limestone and even granite, so that pieces of them crumble away.

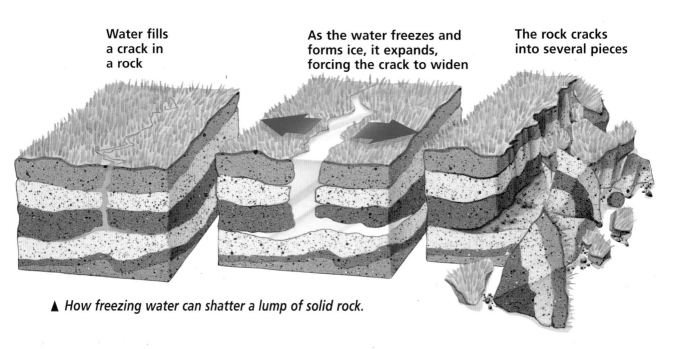

Water fills a crack in a rock

As the water freezes and forms ice, it expands, forcing the crack to widen

The rock cracks into several pieces

▲ *How freezing water can shatter a lump of solid rock.*

Hot days, cold nights

In hot, dry places, such as deserts, the heat during the day makes the rocks expand. At night they cool and **contract**. This gradually causes the rocks to crack, until pieces break off them. Sometimes, as the air cools at dusk, pieces of rock break off with a loud bang that sounds like gunfire.

Plants and animals

This wearing away of rocks, by sun, rain, frost and snow, is known as **weathering**. Plants also wear away rocks. If a tree seed starts to grow in a crack in a rock, its roots grow deeper down into the crack. As the roots grow they force the sides of the crack further apart. This weakens the rock and eventually it may begin to split. Burrowing animals can also widen cracks in rocks and weaken them.

▲ The roof of this house was pulled off as a result of a landslide. The damage was so great that the house was abandoned.

► As the roots of a tree grow into a crack in a rock, they force the sides of the crack apart. Eventually the rock will begin to split.

Landslides in action

Weathered pieces of rock sometimes slide downhill as soon as they break off. But usually the pieces collect in one place until something starts them moving. This can be a natural event such as heavy rains, melting snow, an earthquake or waves from the sea. Humans can start off landslides too, especially by digging **mines** or drilling foundations, which shakes the ground and dislodges rocks.

▼ *The bank of rocky material at the foot of this mountain is called scree. It was formed when rocks high on the mountain were weathered and then rolled down.*

Rock falls

There are three main kinds of landslide involving solid rock – rock fall, rock slide and slumping. In a **rock fall**, fragments of rock, called **scree**, break away from the face of a steep hill, mountain or cliff. They collect at the foot of the slope. After many years they form a cone-shaped pile called a scree slope.

There are many small rock falls on the sides of mountains, especially in the spring when ice that has frozen in cracks in the rock begins to melt, releasing pieces of rock.

Rock slides

In a **rock slide**, a mass of rock moves rapidly down a slope. Rock slides are more dangerous than rock falls because they often occur on lower slopes, where they are nearer to farms and villages. Rock slides have killed many people and destroyed villages in the Canadian Rockies, Norway, Switzerland and in many other mountainous areas.

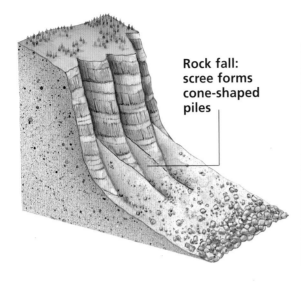

Rock fall: scree forms cone-shaped piles

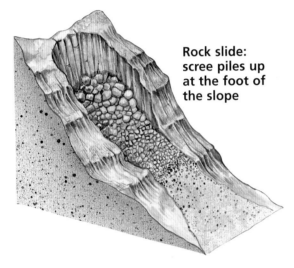

Rock slide: scree piles up at the foot of the slope

▲ Rock slides, like this one in Taiwan, can often cause serious road blocks.

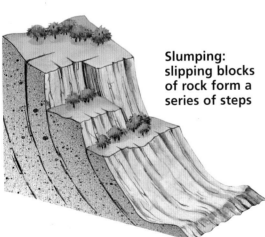

Slumping: slipping blocks of rock form a series of steps

▲ These three kinds of landslide show how lumps of solid rock can move down a slope.

Slumping

Slumping is a landslide where the falling rock moves as a huge block. The block tilts backwards as it slides down a cliff or mountain slope.

Slumping is often set off by an earthquake. It occurs most often where a layer of hard rock, with lots of cracks and joints in it, lies on top of a layer of smoother, slippery rock, such as clay or shale. The slumping blocks of rock may be up to three kilometres long and 150 metres thick. A slump often creates a series of large steps down a slope.

Falling cliffs

Where high ground meets the sea, there are steep rock faces called cliffs. Landslides occur regularly along some cliffs as they are attacked by the sea. The cliffs move slowly inland as powerful waves wear them away.

Wave power

Waves are caused by the wind blowing across the sea and pushing the surface of the water into a series of ridges and hollows.

Waves wear away cliffs in two ways. The first is where water is flung against cliffs by the crashing waves. The water compresses or squashes the air in the cracks and pores in the rocks. When the water flows back, the air in the rock seems to explode, bursting the rocks apart.

During a storm, the force of the waves can be three times greater than normal – powerful enough to shift a piece of rock weighing more than 1000 tonnes. So it is hardly

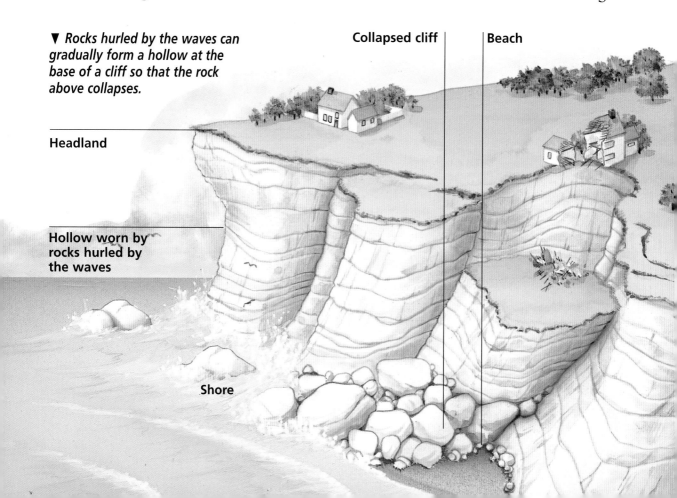

▼ *Rocks hurled by the waves can gradually form a hollow at the base of a cliff so that the rock above collapses.*

Headland

Hollow worn by rocks hurled by the waves

Shore

Collapsed cliff

Beach

surprising that the waves can cause huge pieces of cliff to fall without warning.

Hurled rocks

The waves also hurl rocks and boulders against the lower part of cliffs. This slowly creates a hollow at the base of the cliff. The hollow grows bigger and bigger until eventually there is no base to support the top of the cliff. When the cliff becomes top-heavy, parts of it crash down on to the **beach** below. A flat area of rock, called a **wave-cut platform** is left where the cliff once stood.

▲ *These lumps of rock have fallen from a cliff in the Algarve, Portugal. The waves will slowly break them down into sand and pebbles.*

Coastal features

Some cliffs are made of layers of hard and soft rock. As the soft rocks wear away they form **bays**. The hard rocks are left jutting out as **headlands**. In places where soft rocks are being worn away, cliff falls may mean that large areas of farmland are lost, as well as roads, footpaths and even houses and other buildings. Eighteenth-century maps, for example, show towns and villages along the coast of eastern England that now lie under the sea.

◄ *The top of a cliff crumbles on the east coast of England. In some parts of England, the coastline is being eroded by 25 cm a year.*

Mudslides

Mudslides form when soil or other loose material on a slope is soaked with water. This usually happens after a sudden, very heavy rainstorm or when snow melts rapidly on hills and mountains. Some mudslides are caused by water mixing with the ash from a volcano. The wet material no longer sticks to the slope and slides downwards, flowing like a liquid.

▼ *A mudslide forms when soil or ash on a slope becomes soaked with water.*

Southern Italy

At least 81 people were killed, and many more were injured when mudslides and flooding struck southern Italy in May 1998. Heavy rains in the hills around Naples washed thousands of tonnes of mud down into the valleys below. The mud came from hills where, in the past, trees had been cut down or burned.

The mud rushed down gullies like a tidal wave. It tore down houses and bridges and swept away cars and trees. Parts of some villages were buried under two metres of mud. When the rain finally stopped, the sun baked the mud hard. This made it even harder for rescuers to reach people buried under the mudslide.

Hillside

Rain

Waterlogged soil or ash

Houses engulfed by mudslide

▲ *Soldiers dig for survivors in the mud left by a mudslide that struck Colombia in 1987.*

▼ *Mudslides, caused when the Nevado del Ruiz volcano erupted in Colombia, brought death and destruction to the surrounding area.*

Nevado del Ruiz volcano

Many volcanoes are so tall that they are covered with snow. If the volcano erupts, red-hot ash mixes with the melting snow and forms an extremely dangerous mudslide.

This happened when the Nevado del Ruiz volcano in Colombia, South America, erupted in November 1995. The snow and ice on the volcano melted, and the water carried thousands of tonnes of ash with it as it rushed down the mountainside.

One of the streams of mud was 40 metres high, while some travelled 60 kilometres before they finally came to a halt. Altogether, the mudslides killed more than 23 000 people and destroyed many homes.

Soil creep

During a landslide, thousands of tonnes of rocks and soil can come crashing down the side of a hill or mountain. Whole villages may be buried and many people may be killed or injured.

Much less spectacular is **soil creep**. Although soil creep is slow, it probably carries more soil downhill in a year than all the landslides in the world put together.

Creeping soils

Soil creep occurs when soil slides down a slope so slowly that it is hardly noticeable. Soil creep starts when the soil on a slope is loosened by heavy rain or frost, or by small animals burrowing into it. Animals such as cows and sheep trampling the soil may also cause soil creep. Soil creep occurs even when there are plants covering the ground.

▼ *Soil creep on the slopes of a hill in Starbotton, Yorkshire, England.*

Terracettes

When the soil is held together by plant roots, it moves down a slope in large slabs rather than as tiny particles. These settle into little steps or **terracettes**. Other signs of soil creep are tilting telegraph poles, leaning walls and cracked roads. Trees on hillsides where there is soil creep often have bent trunks. As the soil creep tilts them, the trees grow back towards the sun again.

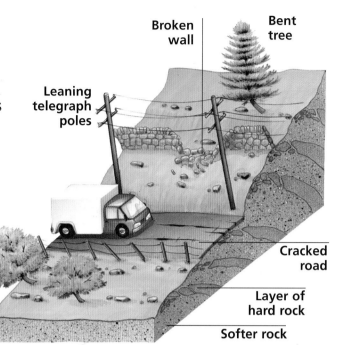

▲ Some of the effects of soil creep.

Problems with soil creep

Soil creep can cause serious problems. The Grand Coulee Dam is a massive concrete **dam** across the Columbia River in the United States. It stands 167 metres high. Work started on the dam in 1933, but as fast as the engineers dug the foundations, wet soil from the surrounding hills slipped into them. Eventually the engineers used huge refrigerators to freeze the wet soil. This stopped the soil from creeping down until the foundations of the dam were finished.

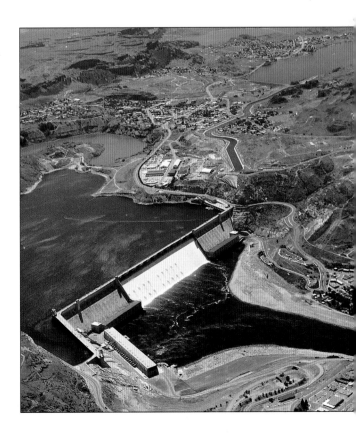

► Soil creep made it difficult for engineers to build the Grand Coulee Dam in Washington State in the United States. The dam was built for flood control, to provide hydroelectric power and to irrigate farmland.

Man-made landslides

Although landslides and mudslides are natural processes, people can make them worse. Digging mines and **quarries** into the sides of hills and mountains, or clearing forests on slopes, can either start a landslide or make one worse than it would otherwise have been.

▼ *Man-made landslides are changing the shape of the Andes Mountains in South America.*

▲ *An irrigation scheme in Guatemala waterlogged the soil, causing this landslide.*

Irrigation

In areas where the soil is poor and dry, farmers use **irrigation** to water their crops. But poorly-planned irrigation schemes on hillsides can cause the soil to become extremely wet so that it starts to slide down the mountain, causing a landslide.

Mining landslides

When mines are dug into hillsides, they make the rocks above unstable. In the Andes Mountains, gold mines are often dug without any planning. When it rains, they flood, and the mountainside is weakened.

After heavy rains in December 1992, hundreds of thousands of tonnes of hillside in Bolivia came hurtling down. The landslide buried the mines and also the miners who were camping in the valley below. More than 1000 people were killed.

▼ *The Panama Canal has to be dredged to remove the material dumped in it by landslides. These are caused by the cutting down of the forests on the banks of the canal.*

Removing forests

Trees help to keep soil in place and make it less likely to slide down a slope. But over many years, people on the islands of Leyte and Negros in the Philippines had cleared the forests on their mountains for timber and firewood. When a **typhoon** struck the islands in November 1991, the soil was no longer held in place by tree roots or protected by the trees and bushes above.

The heavy rain that came with the typhoon washed huge amounts of soil and rock from the mountainsides. The landslides and mudslides blocked roads and destroyed bridges and houses. More than 6000 people died.

Preventing landslides

As we have seen, landslides and mudslides damage buildings and block roads, railways and **canals**. They can also injure or kill people. But there are ways of preventing landslides or of reducing the damage and destruction they cause.

Basins and buildings

People in Los Angeles in the United States have dug huge, stadium-sized basins below the mountains where landslides are likely to occur. These catch the material that falls down from the mountains and stop the landslides damaging property or injuring people. The basins need to be cleared out regularly.

Damage and injury can also be prevented if people are not allowed to build houses on steep slopes where landslides are likely to occur.

Road and railway cuttings

The **cuttings** where roads and railways pass through mountain areas can also cause landslides. Steep-sided cuttings are more dangerous than gently sloping ones. Sometimes shelves or steps are made in the sides of steep cuttings to collect rocks that fall down the slopes.

▲ *The slopes on each side of this road cutting in Scotland have been cut into steps to prevent rock fall. The road leads to the Forth Bridge.*

Overhanging rock faces can be supported by concrete pillars or strengthened with steel rods. Wire mesh is often used to hold loose rock fragments in place. Deep trenches are often dug down a slope in order to divert the water that might cause a landslide. These trenches are then filled with gravel so that they do not collapse or wear away as the water flows down them.

Warnings

A landslide in the city of San Francisco, USA, in 1982 killed 25 people and caused damage costing more than 66 million dollars. After the disaster, the government set up a landslide warning system.

Scientists now collect information about the rainfall, wind speed, slope, kind of rocks and soil conditions in the area. They feed the information into a computer and use it to predict when landslides are likely to occur. Warnings can then be given on radio and television. This information has saved many lives.

▲ *A tunnel has been built along a section of road beneath a bridge to protect traffic on the road from falling rocks from a steep cliff.*

▼ *The main ways of preventing landslides.*

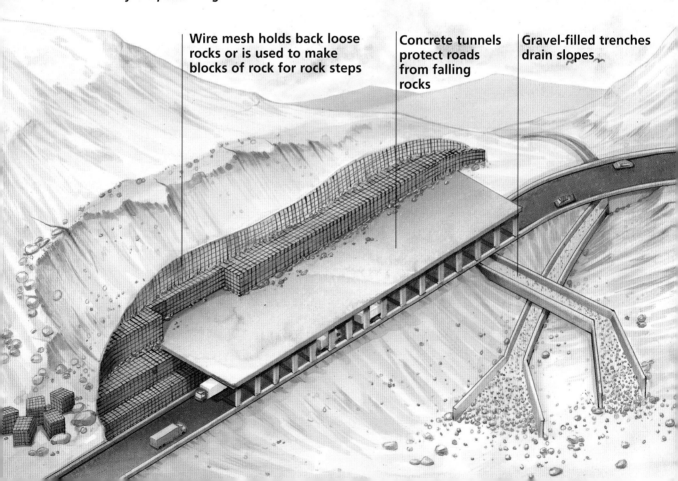

Wire mesh holds back loose rocks or is used to make blocks of rock for rock steps

Concrete tunnels protect roads from falling rocks

Gravel-filled trenches drain slopes

Avalanches

An avalanche is a mass of snow and ice that suddenly crashes down a mountainside into the valley below. An avalanche may be small and simply block a path or sweep away a fence. Or it can be huge, and block roads, knock over trees and bury people and buildings. Many avalanches sweep along chunks of rock, which makes them even more dangerous.

▲ *A scene of devastation after an avalanche swept through the village of Wengen in Switzerland on 8 February 1999.*

A rise in temperature

Avalanches are most common on steep mountain slopes, particularly if there are no trees to hold back the snow. They are more likely to occur when the temperature rises during a spell of warm weather and the winter snow begins to melt. They are also common after a sudden, heavy fall of snow which does not have time to stick to the rock, ice or snow beneath it.

Sudden noises

Several other things can set off an avalanche. An earthquake or a sudden gust of wind may dislodge the snow. A loud noise, such as a car engine backfiring or a gunshot, can start huge masses of snow moving. Even the noise or sudden movement made by a skier can be enough to set off an avalanche.

Once the mass of snow or ice has started to move, it can tumble several kilometres down the mountainside at terrifying speeds, sometimes reaching 320 kilometres per hour. There is usually little or no chance to escape the path of an oncoming avalanche.

Kinds of avalanche

There are two main kinds of avalanche. In very cold, dry weather, light powdery snow grains do not stick together. If this snow starts to move down the mountainside, it forms a **powder avalanche** that swirls along like an enormous white cloud.

A **slab avalanche** starts off as a solid chunk of frozen snow about the size of a soccer pitch and about nine metres thick. It often forms when sunny days are followed by frosty nights and snow that has melted freezes again. Whatever kind of avalanche it is, if it catches up with walkers, climbers or skiers, they have little chance of surviving.

▲ *An avalanche on Mount McKinley, Alaska, in the United States.*

▼ *The two main kinds of avalanche.*

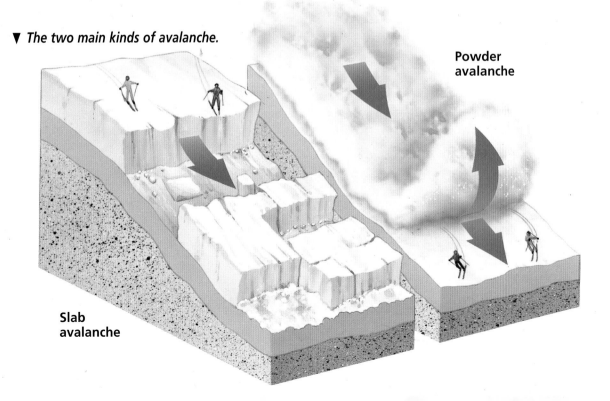

Powder avalanche

Slab avalanche

Dangers and damage

Every year about 100 million people go on holiday to the European Alps. About 150 of them are killed by avalanches. In the United States nearly 500 people have been killed by avalanches since 1950. Wherever there are mountains there is a risk that avalanches will occur.

There is little chance of surviving an avalanche. Many people are killed instantly by the force of the avalanche. About 70 per cent of victims do not survive longer than 20 minutes in the freezing conditions. Trained dogs are used to search for avalanche victims. It takes a dog half an hour to search an area that it would take 20 people four hours to cover.

▲ Rescuers use specially trained dogs to search for avalanche victims.

Double trouble

On 23 February 1999 rising temperatures and showers of rain loosened snow in the Austrian Alps. An avalanche buried the tiny town of Galtür under five metres of snow. Roads were blocked and phone lines were down. For a whole night, rescue helicopters could not reach the disaster zone because of raging snowstorms. The next afternoon, a second avalanche hit the village of Valzur, three kilometres away. Over 400 people and 50 helicopters were involved in the rescue, but only 25 victims were found alive. In all, 38 people lost their lives. It was the worst alpine natural disaster in more than 40 years.

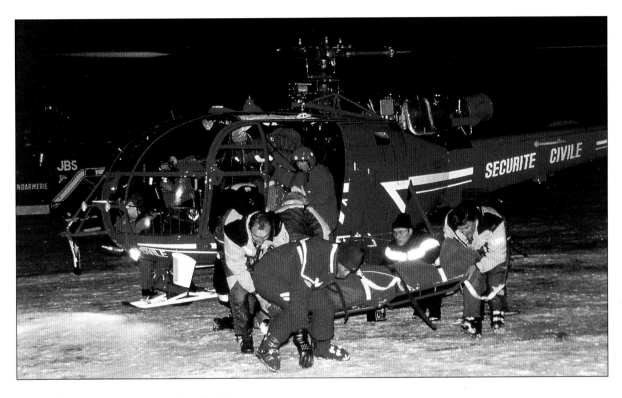

▲ *An avalanche in the French Alps in January 1998 killed 11 people.*

Turkish tragedy

The deadliest avalanches in recent years occurred in Turkey early in 1992. Heavy snowfalls had buried parts of eastern Turkey under more than nine metres of snow. The thick layer of snow on the steep-sided mountains set off avalanches over several days, beginning on 31 January. Whole villages were buried, and hundreds of people were killed. Strong winds, blinding snow and blocked roads made it difficult for rescuers to reach the avalanche victims.

◄ *A helicopter airlifts a person to safety in the Alps. Clear blue skies make it easier for the rescue helicopters to fly.*

Preventing avalanches

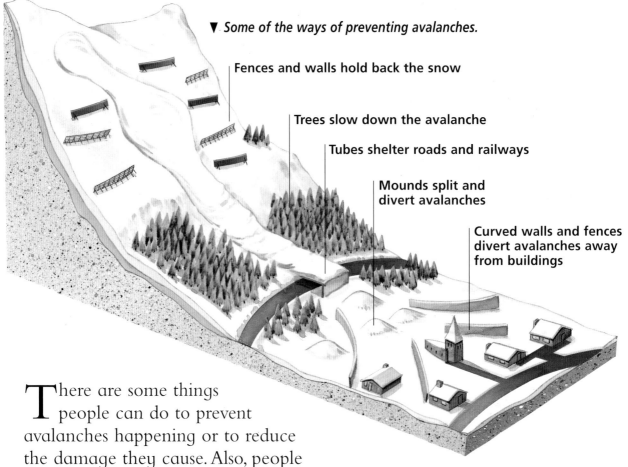

▼ *Some of the ways of preventing avalanches.*

Fences and walls hold back the snow

Trees slow down the avalanche

Tubes shelter roads and railways

Mounds split and divert avalanches

Curved walls and fences divert avalanches away from buildings

There are some things people can do to prevent avalanches happening or to reduce the damage they cause. Also, people who live in or visit mountain areas can be warned when avalanches are likely to occur.

Fences and tubes

Fences made of wood, aluminium or steel can be built on steep slopes where snow collects in deep drifts. If the snow starts to slide, the fences stop it from forming large slabs.

► *These fences made of steel help to break up large slabs of snow during avalanches.*

▲ *In some mountain areas, guns or explosives are used to set off avalanches before they can cause too much damage.*

avalanches. Unfortunately, in many avalanche areas the trees have been cleared for timber or to make ski slopes. In these areas it is difficult for new trees to grow because of the extreme cold, strong winds and avalanches.

Guns and explosives

Instead of waiting for huge amounts of snow to collect on slopes, small, harmless avalanches can be set off by small explosions. In countries such as Switzerland, explosive charges are planted in avalanche areas before winter begins. The explosives are set off during the winter whenever dangerously large amounts of snow begin to build up. A planned, mini avalanche is much easier to deal with than a surprise big one.

Protecting buildings

In avalanche areas the roofs of buildings are often placed level with the slope of the hill. This allows the sliding snow to pass over them harmlessly. Roads and railways are protected by tubes made of concrete, wood or metal.

Forests and trees

Forests of large, mature trees growing on mountain slopes form one of the best protections against

Research

The more we know about the causes of avalanches, the easier it will be to prevent them from happening. In Montana in the United States, for example, scientists have built an underground lookout post on the slopes of a mountain. Using explosives, they deliberately set off an avalanche. As it rushes down the mountain, it passes over the scientists and they can study the avalanche from 'the inside'.

Creeping ice

Ice and snow can tumble rapidly down a mountain as an avalanche. They can also creep down the sides of a mountain, often carrying many thousands of tonnes of rocks and soil with them.

Glaciers

High in the mountains where it is very cold, the snow never melts. As new snow falls, it settles and piles up in hollows called **corries**. There the bottom layers are so squashed that they turn to ice. In time, when the layer of ice is about 30 metres thick, it starts to slide slowly down the mountain. This moving river of ice is called a **glacier**.

▲ Glaciers, such as this one in Argentina, move very slowly. As they move, the rock fragments they carry start to carve out a U-shaped valley.

◄ At the tip or 'snout' of a glacier, the ice melts, forming a river or stream and dumping pieces of rock carried along by the glacier. The loose rock is known as terminal moraine.

Changing the landscape

As the glacier flows down the mountain it picks up loose rocks. More frost-shattered rocks and stones fall on to the glacier from the mountains on either side of it. These too are carried along by the glacier. This debris, called **moraine**, grinds, scratches and scrapes away the rock underneath, and at the sides of, the glacier. It slowly **erodes** the land into new shapes.

Rock glaciers

On high mountains, the insides of the heaps of frost-shattered rocks may stay at temperatures below freezing all the year round. Any rain or melting snow that seeps between the rocks may also freeze.

Sometimes enough ice forms so that the whole mass of rock fragments and ice move downhill like a glacier. This moving mass of rock and ice is called a **rock glacier**.

A rock glacier may be 1500 metres long, 500 metres wide and 30 metres thick. It can travel 150 centimetres a year. When it reaches lower ground, where the weather is warmer, the ice melts. The rock pieces are left as a steep scree slope.

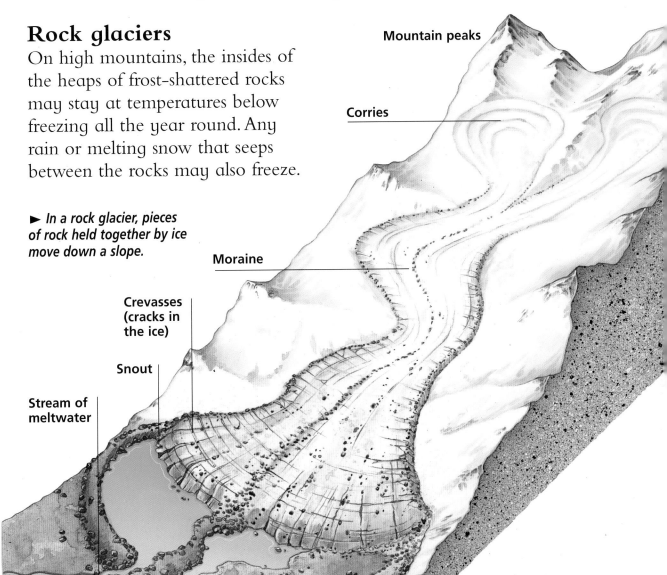

▶ *In a rock glacier, pieces of rock held together by ice move down a slope.*

Mountain peaks

Corries

Moraine

Crevasses (cracks in the ice)

Snout

Stream of meltwater

Past and future

Avalanches and landslides can bring about great destruction. They also kill and injure many people every year. But they do have some uses. Landslides, like glaciers, change the landscape by moving rocks and soil from place to place. And both avalanches and landslides can also teach us about the past.

Ice-age burials

At times in the past, the Earth's climate was much colder than it is now. The most recent of these **ice ages** started about 1.6 million years ago and ended about 11 000 years ago. Avalanches during the ice ages buried some of the people and animals who were living then. Their bodies were **preserved** as if they had been kept in a deep freeze for thousands of years. By studying some of these deep-frozen people and animals, scientists have been able to discover a great deal about life thousands of years ago.

Herculaneum

Herculaneum was a prosperous seaside town on the Bay of Naples in Italy. About 5000 people lived there in AD 79 when the nearby volcano, Mount Vesuvius, erupted. Ash from the volcano, and the mudslides it caused, buried the town in a sea of mud and ash 25 metres deep. Vesuvius erupted again in 1631 and covered Herculaneum with even more ash and mud.

◄ *These giant tusks belonged to a woolly mammoth that was discovered frozen in ice in Siberia. It is at least 10 000 years old.*

Today **archaeologists** are digging away the layers of ash and dried mud to reveal the public buildings, shops, houses and statues as they were on the day Vesuvius erupted in AD 79. Their findings have taught us many details about what life was like in ancient Roman times.

The future

Most scientists believe that our world is getting warmer. **Global warming** is caused by gases put into the air by the increasing number of motor vehicles, aircraft, power stations and factories. Higher temperatures may cause more storms, hurricanes, tornadoes, **droughts**, floods and heavy snowfalls. This could make landslides and avalanches even more common unless we take action to reduce the air **pollution**.

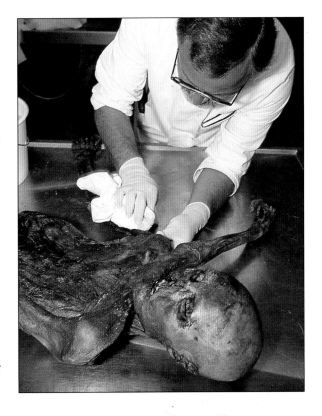

▲ *The oldest complete human body ever found was discovered on the border of Italy and Austria in 1991. The Ice Man dates from 3300 BC.*

▼ *Waste gases from a coal-fired power station rise into the air, adding to global warming.*

Glossary

acidic Containing acid. Acids have the power to soften certain rocks, or even erode them away. Rainwater is slightly acidic.

archaeologist A scientist who finds out about history by digging for clues from the past. Mudslides and glaciers can preserve the remains of plants and animals, including people.

avalanche A sudden fall of snow down the side of a mountain.

bay A place on the coastline where the shore curves inwards.

beach The strip of sand or pebbles between the sea and the land.

canal An artificial waterway.

contract To get smaller.

corrie A steep-sided, crescent-shaped hollow on a mountainside, that has been carved out by a glacier.

cutting The man-made valley that is dug through a piece of high land when a road or railway is being built.

dam A large wall or bank built to hold back water and to raise its level. A large lake called a reservoir often forms behind the dam.

drought An unusually long period of dry weather. Droughts are most typical of places that have a dry season and a wet season.

earthquake A violent shaking of the ground caused when large pieces of rock in the Earth's crust move.

Earth's crust The outer layer of the Earth, made up of huge slabs of rock. Volcanoes and earthquakes may happen where the edges of these rocks wrench apart or grate together.

erode To wear away land. Land is eroded by wind, moving water or ice.

glacier A large river of ice or ice and rock that flows down a valley.

global warming The warming of the Earth caused by gases such as carbon dioxide in the air. These gases reduce the amount of the sun's heat that escapes into space.

headland A piece of land on the coastline that sticks out into the sea.

ice age One of several long, very cold periods in the history of the Earth, when glaciers and ice sheets covered large parts of the northern hemisphere.

irrigation A man-made system for watering crops, often by means of channels dug to divert water from a reservoir.

landslide Soil or rocks sliding down the side of a hill or mountain.

mine A place where coal, metals or other minerals are dug out of the ground.

moraine The pieces of rocks carried along and then dumped by a glacier.

mudslide The movement of a mass of mud down the side of a hill or mountain.

porous Something which allows a liquid or air to pass through it is said to be porous.

powder avalanche An avalanche made up of powdery grains of snow that do not stick together.

pollution Dirty air, water or soil caused by chemicals or gases.

preserved Kept from decaying.

quarry A place where stone, slate, sand or gravel is dug out of the ground.

rock fall Fragments of rock, or scree, that break away from the face of a steep cliff, hill or mountain and collect at the foot of the slope.

rock glacier A slow-moving mass of rock held together by ice that flows down a valley.

rock slide A mass of rock that moves rapidly down a slope.

scree The bank of pieces of weathered rock which collects at the bottom of a steep mountain slope.

slab avalanche An avalanche which consists of a large slab of frozen snow.

slumping When large blocks of rock slip down a slope and settle into a series of giant 'steps'.

soil creep The slow, gradual movement downhill of soil and tiny rock fragments.

terracette A small level strip of land like a step, on the side of a hill.

typhoon A violent windy storm, which is also called a cyclone or hurricane.

valley A low-lying strip of land between steep hills or mountains. A river or stream may run along the bottom of the valley.

volcano A hole or tear in the Earth's crust from which molten rock (lava) or red-hot ashes may be forced out into the air.

wave-cut platform A level area of rock at the base of a sea cliff. It is formed when waves erode the bottom of a cliff, making the top of the cliff collapse.

weathering The breaking up of rocks by heat, cold, ice and rainwater. This process can be speeded up by plant roots pushing the rocks apart or by burrowing animals that loosen fragments of rock.

Index